To Abe, Zeke, and Pete —M.M.

*For Brewster, who was there
from the beginning* —A. G.

Published by Charlesbridge
9 Galen Street
Watertown, MA 02472
(617) 926-0329
www.charlesbridge.com

Library of Congress Cataloging-in-Publication Data
Names: Muirhead, Margaret, author. | Gustavson, Adam, illustrator.
Title: Flip! : how the Frisbee took flight / Margaret Muirhead ; illustrated
    by Adam Gustavson.
Description: Watertown, MA : Charlesbridge, 2019.
Identifiers: LCCN 2018052241 (hardcover) | LCCN 2018053803 (ebook) |
    ISBN 9781632897367 (ebook) | ISBN 9781580898805 (hardcover)
Subjects: LCSH: Flying discs (Game)–Juvenile literature.
Classification: LCC GV1097.F7 (ebook) | LCC GV1097.F7 M65 2019 (print) |
    DDC 796.2--dc23
LC record available at https://lccn.loc.gov/2018052241

Printed in China
(hc) 10 9 8 7 6 5 4 3 2 1

Illustrations were done in gouache on paper
Display type set in Atomatic Com by Johannes Plass of Linotype
    and CC Atomic Wedgie by John 'JG' Roshell of Active Images
Text type set in Chaparral Pro by Carol Twombly of Adobe
Color separations by Colourscan Print Co Pte Ltd, Singapore
Printed by 1010 Printing International Limited in Huizhou, Guangdong, China
Production supervision by Brian G. Walker
Designed by Sarah Richards Taylor and Jon Simeon

For centuries, folks have been flipping for flying discs. Did cave kids reel round rocks? Maybe. Did the most macho of the Ancient Greeks flick discs? Certainly.

But who *really* invented the thrilling, top-selling toy that came to be called the **Frisbee**?

One slice of the story started in the 1920s, when Joseph P. Frisbie, a baker's son, delivered desserts to Yale University in New Haven, Connecticut. The college kids sure polished off those pies. And when they were done, they were left with a stack of empty tins, stamped "Frisbie's Pies."

No one knows who was the first to fling one, but the fun became a fad on campus.

Turns out a great idea can pop up in more than one place.
Fast-forward from Frisbie Pies to 1937 and a kid called
Fred Morrison. What does a high-school football player from
sunny Southern California have to do with those East Coast
flying pie plates? Not much.

Fred didn't know a thing about those pie plates that Thanksgiving. After a belly-bursting feast, he and his girlfriend Lu wandered into the backyard. Someone picked up a flat, tin popcorn lid. Nothing special. Until . . . flicked backhand, the lid dipped, skipped, fluttered, and flew!

From then on Fred was gripped with the need to flip.
Everywhere Fred went he toted that tin lid with him,
ready for a game of toss. He hooked Lu on the habit, too.
After a few dents and dings, though, the popcorn tin
wouldn't fly straight. So Fred and Lu tried pie plates.

Then cake pans—even better.

Before long it wasn't unusual at all to see Fred and Lu flipping a cake pan on the coast of Cali. The beach was a perfect place to play.

"Can I buy that from you?" a sunbather begged Fred one day. "I'll give you a quarter."

Fred made some quick calculations: *I bought that pan for a nickel. That's a twenty-cent profit!* "Sold!" he said. Plus, Fred loved the idea of introducing others to the fun of spinning tin.

Fred had an inkling this new business idea could fly. For a kid low on funds, he figured peddling pans at beaches and public parks was one way to cash in. He got to work.

Fred sold enough cake pans to save up for something special: a thirty-five-dollar engagement ring for Lu. She said yes! In 1939 they were married.

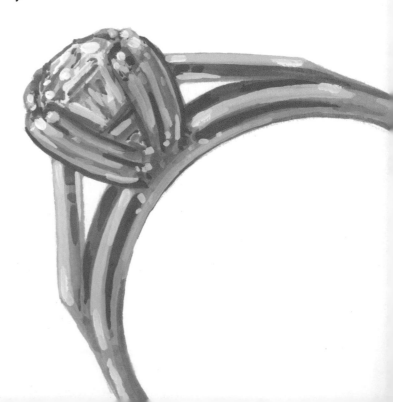

Flying cake-pan sales were good, but Fred was always dreaming up schemes for how to improve his product. Unfortunately, larger events got in the way. In 1941 America entered World War II. A year later, Fred set aside his pan-peddling business plans to serve as an Army Air Corps pilot.

During the war Fred piloted dozens of dangerous missions. As he learned about the basics of flight, his imagination took off, too. What if he designed a flying tin with rounded edges like the wings of his airplane? Or raised ridges like the blades of a turbine? He couldn't forget about those flitting discs!

When Fred arrived home, a growing fad was hovering over America. In 1947, after reports of an alien spacecraft crashing in Roswell, New Mexico, the country went crazy for anything extraterrestrial.

Unexplained Flying Objects? Soaring saucers? Fred had to wonder whether he could connect this outer-space craze with his flying cake-pan obsession.

Fred started looking into different materials he could use to make his pans soar while also withstanding scrapes and scuffs. Light, bright, and pliable plastic was the answer!

Fred introduced his love of flipping and pursuit of space-age material—to a friend and fellow vet named Warren Franscioni. Together they created a plastic disc named the "Flyin-Saucer," in the spirit of the UFO frenzy. With Warren's financial backing, they launched the disc in 1948. Fred pictured the trendy saucers gliding high, with swarms of shoppers lined up to buy them all.

Unfortunately Fred wasn't quite right. In cool temperatures the Flyin-Saucer's plastic became brittle and broke to bits. Fred's hopes were beginning to shatter, too.

But the guy didn't give up. At times he wanted to. But Fred continued to believe his product had promise, if he could just make it better.

In 1955 Fred was ready to try again. This time he had the perfect partner in mind. No one matched Fred's fervor for the flying disc like Lu! Together they set about making a new mold with a more flexible plastic. They would need a new name, too.

"How about something after the most recently named planet?" Fred suggested. "Pluto . . . Pluto Platter?" They liked it!

Sporting a spacesuit that Lu had sewn, Fred began selling Pluto Platters at fairs. The latest plastic model didn't break. Fred and Lu also began performing basic tricks for customers— flat flips, curves, and skips. Crowds began to clamor for their Pluto Platters.

Soon Pluto Platters were flying all over the West Coast. A California toy company took interest. "Could this be the next big thing?" the Wham-O executives wondered. "We should know!" they said. "We're the makers of the Hula Hoop!"

The company met with Fred and Lu and offered
to manufacture and promote their flying discs.
They also promised to place the Pluto Platter at
stores around the country—something Fred and Lu
just couldn't do on their own. Fred liked picturing
even more folks picking up a disc and giving it a flick.

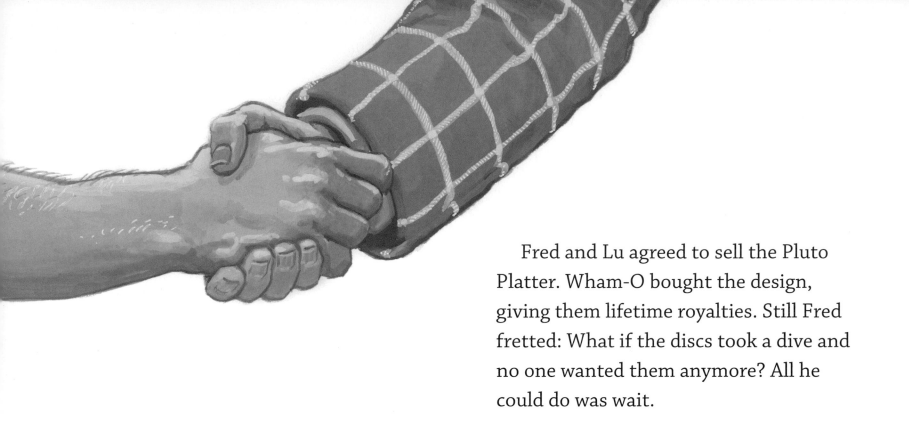

Fred and Lu agreed to sell the Pluto Platter. Wham-O bought the design, giving them lifetime royalties. Still Fred fretted: What if the discs took a dive and no one wanted them anymore? All he could do was wait.

When the Wham-O folks brought the toy to New England, they couldn't believe those kooky college kids already knew how to flip discs! The Wham-O execs also noticed that the students called the Pluto Platters *Frisbies*— a strange name coined after their favorite baker's pie plates.

Wham-O piggybacked on the New England tradition. The company changed the *i* to *e* to rename the Pluto Platter *Frisbee*. Soon sales shot sky-high from the West Coast to the East Coast.

Today Frisbees skim the wind everywhere. More than two hundred million twirl around the world. And many companies produce their own versions of the flying disc.

Fred and Lu were able to retire in style. . . .

But who can we really credit for the Frisbee?
Discus-hurling Ancient Greeks? Pie-craving college
students? Or a California kid who just wouldn't quit?

"Watch out!"

"Heads up!"

"FRISBEE!"